Dedicated To:
Abigail, Nicholas & Baby

Written By: Abigail Gartland

Hello, my name is St. Nicholas!

I was born in Asia Minor in the year 270

Throughout my life, I loved helping people!

One day, I was walking through my town, and I overheard a man saying that he was sad.

I asked him what was wrong, and he said that he didn't have enough money for his family.

I felt sad for him, but I told him that it would be okay as long as he asked God for help!

Late one night, I brought some of my own money to his family.

...and I dropped the money down the chimney of his house so that he would see it in the morning!

Does this story found familiar to you?

It's just like the story of Santa Claus!

Ho ho ho!

Do you know the song called "Jolly Old Saint Nicholas?" That's me!

Do you want to be more like me?

First, you can celebrate my feast day with me on December 6th!

Second, be kind, and go comfort others who are sad.

Third, pray to Jesus to help others who you care about.

Thank you for listening to the story about my life!

I am the patron saint of kids, bakers, and many more things!

I pray for you every day of your life.

St. Nicholas Pray for us!

Copyright:

lipart: © PentoolPixie © LimeandKiwiDesigns
censed purchased: 1/10/2024

About the Author

Abigail Gartland

I love the saints and I love my faith. The idea for sharing the stories of the saints with little ones came when my dear friends were expecting their first baby. I wanted to create something as unique and special as our friendship. Each book is dedicated to very special people and groups who have enriched my faith in different ways. I am blessed to write these stories and appreciate the unending support of my family and friends. When I am not writing, am a middle school teacher. I hope you enjoy these stories. I pray for each and every person who opens one of my books to learn more about the saints.

Abbie

www.ingramcontent.com/pod-product-compliance
Lightning Source LLC
LaVergne TN
LVHW061632070526
838199LV00071B/6656